Thriftology 101

Make money flipping items at thrift store prices for retail profits

Introduction

Thrift stores have gained immense popularity in the last few years. If you haven't heard of the word before, a thrift store is a kind of store with the most unique and commonly used items that are considered second hand. Thrifting is the practice of buying some of the most amazing variety of items at thrift stores and customizing them as per your needs. You can often find name brand clothing, incredible and hard to find antique furniture pieces and just about anything else that you may find at a retail store. If you want to make the most of your invested money and get some unique or high end name brand items at surprisingly cheap prices, you can get great deals on some of the hard-to-find items and have fun browsing through aisle after aisle of items can only be described through the actual experience and thrill of the hunt.

Apart from various online businesses available today, thrifting stores are a great way to make money. As you can find merchandise for almost 99% discount off the normal retail price of the goods, and about 75% off the normal retail prices, one can easily make some good profit by selling these items. You can make high profits every day if you know what and how to buy. This guide is designed to help you understand various attributes around thrifting so that you can easily make some money flipping items at thrift store prices for some retail profits.

Chapter 1 - What is thrifting and

benefits of thrifting?

Humans have been natural gatherers since the beginning of time. We gather more than what we require and with the present constraints of storage, it becomes impossible to have and store as much as we want. Thus, people often choose to donate their clothes or resell them at fractional prices. These donated clothes can be easily bought from the thrift stores and the resold clothes from the resale shops. You would commonly find varied types of clothes from major brands and designer boutiques at the thrift shops. Some of the larger thrift stores have sections of clothing categorized for men, women and children. You can easily browse through them and find the best ones that suit your requirements and specifications. You can even find books, appliances, dishes, toys, furniture, linen and decorative items. You can practically find anything at a thrift store and sometimes the things that people just give away will surprise you. The best part of the whole thrifting experience is that they never run out of their goods. People keep on donating and thrift store managers keep on gathering these items at their stores. So don't get surprised to see the new collection each time to visit a thrift store as the store managers keep their collection updated by bringing in new stocks of donated goods. You will always find new and exciting things at the shops, so keep checking it out periodically so that you don't miss out on some great deals. And if you come across something good, then don't lose the opportunity, just grab it and get the best items at fractions of their sale prices.

One of the most appreciative facts about the thrifting practice is that whatever you pay for the clothes and other items, most of it goes to charity. The manager is responsible for selling the donated items to the general public and the profits made from the sale is donated to local charity groups and associations, which work towards making a difference in our society. Obviously the charitable practice is not followed by all the thrift stores but some of the popular chains like Goodwill and Salvation Army donate parts of their profits for socially beneficial causes.

Thrifting is basically finding and buying costly stuff at their fractional prices from thrift stores. The first thrift store started during the 1800's when the British noble families used to donate their apparel and other belongings to charitable trusts. The idea lived on and today thrift stores are present all over the world. Most of the thrift stores are associated with social causes and charitable organizations. The shops fund these charitable organizations from their profits. You can find churches and other charitable organizations organizing thrift stores for a short period to raise money for social causes. It is true that most of the time you will find used materials and goods but sometimes, if you are lucky, you may find a brand new piece of furniture or clothing with the price tag still intact. Clothing and books are often the most common stuff that you can find at a thrift store. You can also find online thrift stores that work exactly like the retail online stores. You can even find online stores that provide home delivery but the prices may be a bit higher than the ones that don't.

Thrifting has numerous benefits, particularly when you are have limited budget and want to make great profits. You can easily find great deals on relatively new or branded products. Thrifting will only add to your profits and will allow you to stock better things at cheaper prices. The deals are always awesome and discounts you get on the stuff are unmatched. Even the ecommerce sites that deal directly with the manufacturers can't provide such discounts on their products. All the stuff you find there are often in good condition as the managers don't accept or store damaged products and materials. You can aim to make maximum profits from these purchases by buying good quality items for throw-away prices. Another factor that plays an important role here is your negotiation skills. If you can negotiate better, you can make much more than you can imagine. You will often notice that during early mornings and when new stocks arrive, hundreds of people fight to get the best stuffs for themselves. The battle is in itself enthralling, as everyone wants the best at the cheapest prices and the sooner and harder you grab, the better chances you have to own the product.

If you know where to find the best thrift stores in your locality, you can make hundreds of dollars every month. Sometimes the stores are only hit and miss. One day you might find great quality clothes and the next day you won't find any of the ones you had selected the previous day. Most of the time people keep on waiting for days and months to get clothes that suit their requirements. That is why you should never go to a thrift store empty pocket. You never know what great material you may stumble upon.

If you know the right thrift stores, you will find clothes, which are donated by people, are often checked for stains and holes or any other irreparable damages before they are put to sale. So, you will hardly find any damaged clothing at the thrift stores. Make use of this opportunity and buy good quality stuff that you can easily sell for retail profits but now the question that arises is - from where and how to pick such items.

Chapter 2 - What type of thrift stores are best to source at?

Before you understand what types of thrift stores are best to buy your stock from, you need to understand the difference between the types of second hand shops present in our locality. Understanding what they sell and how they gather their materials will help you in understanding where you can find the right products at the best prices. You will find 4 types of second hand sale shops in the market. They are: pawn, consignment, classified and thrift.

Pawn stores are exquisite stores that have the best collection of antique and rarely found items. They sometimes cost more as the objects are hard to find. You can find antique furniture and jewelry that was made hundreds of years ago and are still preserved by their owners. The pawn shops directly work with their owners to sell their products and make very good commission on the sales.

The consignment shops sell for a very short period and often you can find huge discounts on each of their products. They generally put up shop for 2-4 days until their products are sold. They then wait until they have again collected relevant items to be sold.

Classified shops are the ones that sell their clients products directly to the customer without any middleman charges. They are often profitable and generally sell anything they can get their hands on. They charge a nominal fee to place the ads in the newspapers.

Thrift shops work on donations. Often people from higher classes of society donate their unused stuff and the thrift shop owners sell them at fractional prices. They often sell their products at the lowest prices compared to the above types of second hand sale shops.

There are different types of thrift stores that operate throughout the world. The most common ones are the chain thrift stores that have multiple stores in nearly every city. They collect their products in the form of donations from select communities and sell them at lower class areas of the society. You can also find rejected clothing from major manufacturers. The rejected clothing and objects are hardly damaged and can easily be reused by anyone.

Often companies and manufacturers create test products that they have to show to their clients. Once their clients have approved the trial batch, they start production according to their requirements. This trial batch of products is often given away to these chain thrift stores as they enter in to agreements with them. You can easily get these quality branded clothing and other products at throwaway prices if you can make it to the stores at the right time.

You can also find independent and family run thrift stores that always focus on collection quality unused items in their area and sell the products in some other locality. These thrift stores are often profitable as they always have good quality products although they may have been used by their previous owners.

Sometimes you can find antique thrift stores that only sell vintage products. They do not collect other normal products that are easily available at other thrift stores. These are the best stores to find stuff to decorate your house or to get some antique gift for your friends. Unlike pawn shops they do not charge much as they always collect antique items donated by people.

Chapter 3 - Where to locate Thrift stores in and around your area? (Online and other resources)

Finding a thrift store in your area is not so difficult. All you need is a little bit of research and reviews to get to the best thrift stores in your locality. Although, thrift stores may be only concentrated in a particular area where they could make enough sales and get the required exposure among the public, sometimes chain thrift stores are present in most of the localities. You can also find the best thrift stores in the most affluent communities as they donate a lot and most of them are usable by anyone. Sometimes thrift stores are also located just miles outside the cities so that people can travelling can easily get better stuff at cheaper prices. You can always use the internet to find the best thrift stores but sometimes temporary thrift stores that put up shop in selected areas are not mentioned anywhere on the web. Even if they are, by the time you get there, all the best items would have already been sold. So, you need to remain updated through every possible medium to find the best thrift stores in your city. Recommendation from friends and family is always the best way to find the best information about local thrift stores. But if you don't have any colleagues who are interested in thrift stores then follow the below guidelines to find the best thrift stores in your locality.

Firstly, make use of the great social media networking sites; whenever people buy something they tend to post pictures or tweet about it. Follow the commonly used tags about thrifting and you can easily track down every tweet or facebook post that anyone makes on the whole of the web. Thus use some tag follower or even google alerts to track major keywords so that you get an email as soon as google crawls over something related to thrifting. This will not only keep you updated but also ahead of the curve.

Next step is to track down all the major thrift stores in your locality through some local guide or some online guide. Visit them to know more about them and grade their quality of material. This would help you differentiate the good ones from the bad ones. Once you have kept yourself abreast of all information relating to thrift stores, be ready to visit the stores when you find the tweet or the post on any social network.

Chapter 4 - What tools of the trade will you need?

Selecting the right tools to track down and buying the best products from some of these good thrift stores is very important. A collection of applications, websites and directories that contain all information about thrift stores is highly necessary to keep yourself ahead of the curve. The list of mobile applications that would prove to your best ally while buying from thrift stores are:

Thrift Buddy: It is the most comprehensive directory available for the apple device. With more than 10k stores listed in all over the United States, it provides an easy access to all information related to thrift shops and also has genuine reviews from the thrift shop users.

Thrift Shop Locator: it is one of the most popular apps for the android device. It lists all types of thrift shops, consignment shops and flea markets in the whole of US. It has more than 10k listings and also allows you to add your own local listings to the directory.

Thethriftshopper.com: The site works as a thrift shop directory that has the largest listing of the best and the worst thrift stores in the US and all over the world. Each of the users reviews their thrift shop they have visited and the site is full of genuine reviews from thousands of buyers. These reviews could greatly help you form the right decisions about you next thrift shop visit, so that you can buy the good to make the best profits.

Profit Bandit: In order to make the profits on the items you bought at the thrift stores on major auction sites or on your own site, this app could greatly help you compare the original prices of the products, which will further help you decide how much you should actually pay before buying a thrift item

Thrift Town: Another awesome app for the apple devices, it provides clear and precise information about the Thrift Town chain thrift stores. You can also find stock arrivals and shop online from their collection of goods and inventory.

Chapter 5 - How can you decide what you will stock?

Once you have decided on where you intend to buy your items from and have the tools required to start selling, you will need to start getting your stock together.

There are several ways of deciding what you want to buy. Many sellers take the ROI route whilst others prefer to see if the actual profit is worth their time and effort. For instance, some would prefer an ROI of 50% on an item worth $300 but would not waste their time over a 100% ROI on a $2 item.

- If you are spending lots of time on research, correspondence, travel etc, buy items where your ROI will be higher and vice versa.
- Another way of deciding what to buy could depend on what you would like to earn for an hour of work. Think of the wages you would have earned per hour in a job. If that is your goal, buy accordingly. Work out what will be the handling time of selling the item, including travel, cleaning, shooting pictures, posting on the e-commerce site (title, description, deciding the price take time), packaging and shipping/delivery. If for example, it takes you 3 hours to do all this, and you want at least $20 per hour, see if this item will earn you a profit of $60.
- Also remember that you are going to have to pay the web platform from where you sell, the payment gateway that you will use and shipping

and packaging. Will the item you buy earn you enough to cover all these costs?

- How long is this item going to sit on your shelf? Think bank interest – if the item sells immediately, your money returns to you as soon as you invest it. But if you feel that there may not be too many takers for it, should you be buying it?
- Sometimes, volume items are worth the effort. Nobody buys just one plate. So if you are getting the entire set, you may get a better price.
- Where you are going to sell the item may decide whether to buy or not. If it a flea market, a $5 profit may be lucrative, but if you plan to sell it on a website such as eBay, $5 would mean negative earning, thanks to overheads. Also, items that can be easily and more inexpensively shipped may be a better deal if you are working online.

Once you have zeroed in on that particular item in the thrift shop that you hope to flip, examine the product thoroughly. See if the item meets the following criteria:

Clothes:

- All seams, buttons and zippers are intact.

- The cloth is not ripped and has not been darned or mended.
- The cloth is not worn or faded.

Toys and games:

- All pieces are intact.
- No missing pieces in jigsaw puzzles or Scrabble.
- The soft toys are not torn or oozing cotton.

Computer games:

Make sure the cds/dvds work.
- If sealed, check for system requirements. For instance, DOS based games may not run in newer machines.

Glassware/crockery/flatware/silverware:

- Chipped tableware will be difficult to sell.
- Try to get complete sets unless you feel that the piece you are looking at is an antique.
- If the set of spoons is not shiny, do not worry. It most probably is sterling silver. Usually, silver articles have a stamp that will help you figure out whether they are really silver.

Antiques/paintings/frames/jewelry:

- You may not be able to date them or prove their authenticity at that moment. Buy them! In case you do not find that they are of very great value, you can always re-donate.

- If you are focusing entirely on these items, it would be useful to visit museums and libraries and read up on what is authentic.
- A visit to various e stores will also give you an idea what people will pay for such stuff and whether the asking price is worth the effort.

If the items are packed, try and make sure that the box contains what the label reads. If there is a scannable barcode, see product description as per the bar code. Any app similar to Profit Bandit will be helpful. And remember to shop in nicer neighborhoods. They have better salaries and hence more disposable income.

What not to spend your money on

- A designer handbag with a 'Made in China' label.
- Stuff that is too damaged or torn
- Clothes with missing buttons, damaged zippers and worn our collars
- Chipped tableware
- Used bed linen, bath linen, innerwear, bath suits, mattresses and pillows and wigs would

most probably never sell. Don't waste your money and time!

Chapter 6 - Quick Action Guide – A step-by-step plan to get started

So now you have decided that flipping thrift store items is for you. This step-by–step guide will help you navigate the DOs and DONTs of starting a flipping business.

1) The first thing is to get you a smartphone if you don't already have one and start doing research. See what items are being sold on sites like ebay, amazon, craigslist, etc. See what is popular with the buyers and what they are willing to pay for it. Check their terms and conditions and

find out how much they charge towards shipping. Once you have done that, draw out a list for yourself that will help you focus on things that you are interested in selling. After all, each product that you upload on these sites must have a nice title and a well written description. If you are not excited about an article you are trying to sell, it shows!

2) Visit museums and libraries and learn about antiques and paintings. You never know when you will walk on to a great buy and ignore it just because you did not recognize its value.

3) Research thrift stores, garage sales and flea markets in your area. Check what they sell. Compare prices and quality and decide which ones fit your budget since all inventory must be value for money. Every dollar you spend must reflect on the product.

4) Register yourself on web platforms such as eBay and Amazon. They have several forms to be filled and ask questions regarding your citizenship status and bank details so as to ensure that your taxes are reflected properly.

5) Register for a paypal account or its alternatives such as Google Wallet, Wepay, 2Checkout, Authorize.Net, Skrill and many others out there. Make sure you enter all your details correctly. You do not want all your earnings

disappearing due to wrong bank account details.

6) Now for the capital investment – You have already got your smartphone. There are several apps that you need to download. All ecommerce sites now have a mobile app. These apps allow you to buy and sell without having to be in front of your desktop or laptop. So you can click pictures of your product and upload them directly using the mobile apps. Then apps such as the Profit Bandit and Scanpower will help to figure out how much the item you have your eye on will sell for on, say Amazon.

7) The next thing you need to get yourself is a shipping scale that will help you calculate how much you will be spending on shipping. An average scale costs between $12 to $18.

8) To help you with your listing, USB barcode scanner is ideal and will allow you to get through the process really fast. This will cost $10-15 on eBay or Amazon.

9) Buy packaging material such as bubble wraps and brown paper. Save any old boxes and thermocol fillers. A printer will be helpful too. Saves you the time of having to write out all the addresses!

A space to operate from, even if it the garage will be good. Make sure it is only yours!

10)   Open your telephone directory and find a logistics company close to your place of work. Make time to call them and find out the rates for delivery. See if you can get them to pick up the package from your place. That way, you will not be wasting time driving down to their office every time. As your business picks up, so will theirs. So they will be happy to support you and maybe also offer you credit and/or discounts at a later date. These guys are crucial to your venture. So play nice!

11) Now, that you are ready to take off, it is the time to start building your inventory. Using all the information you have got so far, start buying stuff. Remember all the DOs and DONTs. Remember what sells and what does not. Make sure you have checked the item as we   discussed   earlier.

Once you have bought it, see if needs any attention – does it need some polishing, or maybe some buttons need to be reaffixed, or does that designer bag need the zip fixed. Get that sorted before you take pictures.

12)   Ensure that you photograph the product at its most flattering. So a decent table cloth and ample lighting is essential.

13)   Think of an enticing title. The secret is to make a potential buyer curious about your product and you need him to click to open the next page. Once the title is ready, start on the description. Be honest without being off putting. A 'Made in China' Gucci is only a rip-off. So be sure you don't mislead your buyer. He will never buy from you again and most probably destroy your ratings with a disastrous review. An example:

Well preserved bone china dinner set for 4 places
Beautiful bone china dinner set with a delicate floral design in white and blue for sale at an unbelievable price. Includes 4 quarter places, 4 half plates, 4 dinner plates, 2 medium sized serving bowls and a large platter.

Your picture must bear out whatever you write. So make sure all the pieces of the set are there in the picture. In case you are describing clothes, include exact measurements. Study other listings for similar products and try to use the keywords which will help the buyer reach your listing.

14) Done! You are ready to upload your product for sale. But have you decided the price? Using the methods we spoke about in previous chapters, price your product. For instance, how long did it take you to reach this stage for this product? If it took you 5 hours, and you want $10 for an hour of your time, price it accordingly. Factor in the website's commission, the payment gateway's cut and shipping. Decide shipping on the basis of weight and location. So once the buyer enters a pincode, the website can automatically decide shipping costs. Also check out the competition. If someone is selling something similar for even a few cents lesser, your seller may be swayed. If you are sure your product is better, you may want to stick to your guns.

15) Once you have got the price worked out, list your product! And wait!

16) When you receive your first sale, do curb your exuberance! You need to ship it within 24 hours. So start packing your product. Get the address right. Make sure you have added the telephone number of the buyer right so your

courier/logistics company can make sure they are at home when they deliver. Get the courier company to pick up the package or drop it off at their office yourself.

And now you can breathe! You have officially completed your first sale!

Chapter 7 - Where can you sell your products?

A good place to sell your stuff is the online e-commerce stores. Given below are a few e-stores to get you started:

- www.ebay.com
- www.cquot.com

- www.quibids.com
- www.amazon.com
- www.ebid.com
- www.overstock.com
- www.dhgate.com
- www.aliexpress.com

Apart from online stores, other places that attract the kind of clientele you are looking for are garage sales, flea markets and some brick and mortar stores that are looking to capitalize on sales.

A short note on the pros and cons of several websites:

- Some websites transfer you money immediately while others pay weekly. Some use payment gateways, while others like craigslist deal in cash.

- Listing on some sites takes long and some others, which allow you to scan barcodes, the time taken is much shorter.

- Sites like eBay allow you sell via auctions, especially when you are not sure of the price.

- Some sites have exorbitant fees and a 10% off from your earnings can hurt.

- Where the website does not have a payment gateway and you need to collect cash from your buyer, it means that you have to meet him. And that takes time! Moreover, you cannot have customers too far away from you.

Chapter 8 - Terms of the Trade:

Like all other trades, thrifting too has its own jargon. Most of the words however may not be found in your regular dictionary. Here is a list to help you through:

Thrifting: Shopping in thrift stores/flea markets/basement bargain stores for trendy, vintage clothing and/or other items.

Flip: Selling something that you bought for a low price at a higher price in order to make a profit out of it.

Barcode: An image comprising of black and while vertical stripes that stores information about the product you buy from a super market

Barcode scanner: An instrument that helps the check out person scan the barcode in order to read the information stored and convert it into an amount that figures on the bill.

ROI: Short for Return on Investment, and not a term exclusive to thrifting, this lets you know in percentage terms how much you will receive as profit as ratio of money spent.

Garage sale: A sale of articles cleared from the garage or home and put up in the yard for sale. One man's garbage can always be another man's treasure!

Flea Market: Open usually on Saturdays and Sundays, a low priced market where you may get bargains, especially clothes, for throwaway prices.

E-store/e-commerce store/platform: Used to refer to a website where you can buy and sell things online.

Payment Gateway: A service provided by a financial company to make it convenient to pay directly from your credit/debit card for goods or services purchased online.

Conclusion:

Like everything else, thrifting has to be taken seriously in order to make money. While it allows you the independence to live life and earn on your terms, you need to understand that unlike other jobs, you are not covered under any statutory benefits. So insurance and healthcare facilities will not exist as also tax returns till such time that the websites where you are selling your products do not issue a certificate.

However, it allows you to do what you most probably love most. Root through bargain stores, but things cheap and sell them for a profit. The money you earn is a reward for doing all the hard work of getting the product to the buyer without him putting too much effort.

Check Out & Profit From My Other Books

Below you'll find some of my other popular books that are popular on Amazon and Kindle as well. Simply click on the links below to check them out.

How To Make Money Online

http://www.amazon.com/gp/product/B00S6TOJ5Y

The YouTube Manifesto

http://www.amazon.com/gp/product/B00WBVXHLA

Pick It, Flip It & Thrift It

http://www.amazon.com/gp/product/B00T25NSSK

Thriftology 102

http://www.amazon.com/gp/product/B00YWFJD2A

If the links do not work, for whatever reason, you can simply search for these titles on the Amazon website to find them.

CPSIA information can be obtained
at www.ICGtesting.com
Printed in the USA
LVHW081021130622
721126LV00011B/552